SOMETIMES...

SOMETIMES...

A SIMPLE MAN'S COLLECTION OF THOUGHTS AND LESSONS, SOME LIVED/SOME LEARNED

Matt McClure

PALMETTO
P U B L I S H I N G
Charleston, SC
www.PalmettoPublishing.com

© 2024 by Matt McClure

Cover design idea by Makenzie McClure

All rights reserved.

No portion of this book may be reproduced, stored in a retrieval system, or transmitted in any form by any means–electronic, mechanical, photocopy, recording, or other–except for brief quotations in printed reviews, without prior permission of the author.

Paperback ISBN: 9798822964402
eBook ISBN: 9798822964419

"If you bring forth what is within you, what you bring forth will save you; if you do not bring forth what is within you, what you do not bring forth will destroy you."

—Gnostic Gospel of Thomas

Dedicated to:

Makenzie and Jackson, my two greatest achievements in life. Thank You for letting me be your dad. I love U Awful!!

Kristin, my river; warm, strong and always guiding me forward. You have the gift of meeting anyone, no matter where they are at, and never leaving them where you found them.

My Mom. The true rock and source of strength, character and integrity of our family. Your example of always getting back up before the final bell is the inspiration that has pulled me out of the darkness.

Sometimes...We're born into this world with either a silver spoon in our mouths, hiking boots on our feet, or a shovel in our hands. Where we go from there is predicated on whether we depend on others to get us what we want or start climbing and digging our own way out.

Sometimes...That silver spoon becomes like a feeding tube of survival; no matter how hard you try, you just can't seem to wean yourself off the easy life. Thus, your life and your relationships are inherited and never cultivated. The finish line is always visible, and its emptiness is cluttered with the toys accumulated over the years. However, he who dies with the most toys still dies, but he also dies alone and remorseful of a life worth living that was wasted.

Sometimes...Those hiking boots and shovels are some of the greatest gifts known to man. "Lace 'em up" early and continue moving forward, and when necessary, a sidestep or a step back before you regroup and return to your path. Unfortunately, some people will never put the boots on, or if they do, they're just content standing still, or they place them on the wrong feet and spend a lifetime going in circles.

Sometimes...Whether in games on a field, a court, or in this game we call life, you're going to lose. This does not mean you are a loser! Anytime you step on, step up, or step out and choose to compete, you've already won. Maybe not that game or event, but you've won by deciding to get off the sidelines and into the action.

Sometimes...Show me someone who screams and shouts from the sidelines, and I'll show you someone who never got in the game themselves, or if they did, they're now expecting you to achieve the prominence they falsely believe was stolen from them. Play for you and your team and no one else.

Sometimes...You're going to have to fight a battle more than once, not to win, but just to prove your worth and walk away.

Sometimes...You're going to flat out "Lose Yourself." The mind is like a blade of steel; when it's been neglected, it grows dull. To become sharp again, we might have to travel to the most unexpected places. The reason we get lost in the first place is by design, so we can find the path back to who we really are.

Sometimes...If you take a moment to sit alone and do nothing but close your eyes, breathe deeply, and listen to nature...you'll simultaneously cleanse your mind and feed your soul, and that's a damn good day.

Sometimes...The safest and happiest place you will ever encounter is home, no matter what or where that is.

Sometimes...You're going to make a mistake and not be as honest as you should be. This does not mean you are a mistake or dishonest as much as being human. The key is to learn from these transgressions and be a better human.

Sometimes...You're going to fail. WE ALL DO! Most folks are overly concerned with whether they failed big or failed small. The real key is whether you learned big or small from your failures. Failure is a superior professor of success.

Sometimes...Someone is going to tell you you're not as good as you think you are. This might be a disingenuous parent, sibling, teacher, or coach. Conversely, those same someone's might also tell you you're so much better than you really are. The motivations are the same, and neither include you nor your best interest. Your happiness resides in you and your ability to see and know the difference.

Sometimes...We find ourselves in unpleasant or dangerous situations because we make decisions and choices based on assumptions because we lack the courage to ask questions instead.

Sometimes...Only when we let go of the man we were can we become the man we know we are destined to be.

Sometimes...You're going to find yourself broken and seemingly beyond repair. You're not alone; new members are admitted every minute of the day. The fact is you've already acknowledged and accepted you're broken in some form or fashion, and only then can the repair process commence.

Sometimes...No matter how fast or how far you run, at the end of the day, you cannot outrun or run away from you. Wherever you go, patiently waiting for you will be the "stuff" you're trying to leave behind. Constantly running away can lead to physical stamina, but it will only end in mental and emotional exhaustion.

Sometimes...We need to embrace the immense differences between having character and always acting like and being one.

Sometimes...A sedentary approach to taking chances can be fatal. When we dare to move and act, we might lose our traction momentarily, but when we resist that chance to move and act, we risk losing ourselves forever.

Sometimes…An apology without action is merely manipulation, and taking action without insight is likely to only lead to temporary change.

Sometimes…Rather than asking, "Why was I fired? Why did they break up with me? Why didn't I get the promotion?" instead ask: "Why was I fire-able? Why was I breakup-able? Why was I not promotable?"

Sometimes…We have the tendency to depreciate and belittle the significance of the delayed response to our actions, giving far less attention to what can occur in the future compared to the events of today.

Sometimes…You're going to find yourself lying flat on your back and looking up at who, what, and where you really want to be. The stumbles and falls have many faces: promiscuity, alcohol/drugs, divorce, possibly a criminal act, etc. Don't focus on who's trying to help you back up as much as the method in which they're using. Are they throwing you a thick and knotted rope or a slew of dental floss?

Sometimes…We spend far too much of our valuable time looking behind and wallowing in the past. If we continue to always be focusing on yesterday, we'll eventually be stuck there and never have a happier tomorrow.

Sometimes…You will hear people talk about how hard, painful, or too difficult something is to achieve. Whether it is getting into shape, putting down an old habit, earning a college degree, advancing their career, or dipping their toes into a whole new world of discovery and personal growth. These folks are 1000 percent accurate! If it was easy, EVERYONE would be doing it, which makes it that much more rewarding to accomplish.

Sometimes…We are going to be physically exhausted and emotionally drained and not want to do all the things we need to do in order to improve ourselves and be better at what we've chosen to do. Be it on the playing surface, classroom, or boardroom, it doesn't matter. The thing to remember is that out there somewhere is someone else of our equal ability and skill set who is doing all those things today to enhance their ability, despite their mood or energy levels. One day, we will both go head-to-head, and they will have the advantage.

Sometimes…You might find yourself in a situation where you feel trapped with no conceivable way out. In basketball terms, this is what happens when defenders seemingly have us "boxed in" and on the verge of a turnover. Coaches teach us to "pivot" away from the defenders and create a new and safer way in which to advance the ball forward. Life is similar! Pivoting away from trouble is not surrendering; it's a way to create a new vision in order to better see new solutions.

Sometimes...Whoever coined the phrase "enough is enough" was a quitter! When you think that you have exhausted all solutions, there are ALWAYS more options just waiting to be considered.

Sometimes...When we're inebriated or high, we might say empty and mean-spirited things to our loved ones. That's because a broken man's mind only worsens when he indulges. If you stop indulging, you might still be broken. However, if you seek out assistance and take the necessary steps to become unbroken, you'll also stop indulging.

Sometimes...You might be driving in the car with your family one day and hear a song playing from your past, and it's going to bring back some memories and a smile to your face. The reason you're smiling is because, although you greatly appreciate your past, you don't live there anymore.

Sometimes...We seem to "find" the time to do the things we really want to do. Most of us, yes, even the busiest of us, have more than enough available time, but what we lack is a strong sense of what to do with it. Eventually, we fill the void with something frivolous or nonessential, and "poof," there's no more time.

Sometimes…We will encounter certain folks who categorically believe EVERYTHING they think to be righteous and absolute and beyond reproach. Any attempt at enlightenment is futile and a complete waste of time and oxygen.

Sometimes…There will always be those people who continuously bring up and talk about our past failures and misdeeds. This is not intended to remind us, because we have clearly not forgotten any of them. They do this for one reason only—in hopes of getting others to feel less about us in order for them to feel better about themselves.

Sometimes…Despite the difficulty of doing so, we MUST stop holding on to people, places, and things that only hold us back.

Sometimes…Your circle will decrease in size, but it will also increase in value. It's not necessarily because you don't care for or like someone as much as with all the positive changes you've made; there is no longer any room for them.

Sometimes…The folks outside your circle will talk to you in their free time, but your circle will always free up time to talk with you.

Sometimes…You will never know the true strength of your circle until your circle has gone to war together.

Sometimes…When it comes to what we want to attempt or accomplish next, it's best to "keep our cards close to the vest." Our critics can only critique what they think they know.

Sometimes…Our words are like currency. Don't spend them on people who completely lack the capacity to listen and comprehend them.

Sometimes…We need to resist the temptation of picking up the weight for someone who is more than capable of doing it themselves, or soon, we'll be loading our backs with that individual as well.

Sometimes…Over the course of our lives, we might lose some material things, but we really didn't lose anything at all. We also, at some point, whether due to neglect or dietary choices, experience some sort of health scare and quite possibly lose something very precious. But if at any point in our journey we lose or compromise our character, then we have truly lost our value.

Sometimes…Our personal issues and struggles are like a hard rainstorm. Eventually a rainbow appears, but we still might have to crawl through some mud to appreciate it.

Sometimes…Ruminating on our issues only manifests them and thus leads to more pain, which leads to more rumination and then more pain, so forth and so on. Make a conscious effort to "get up and move," preferably outside. You might be amazed when you return: although your issues are still there where you left them, your desire to continue to ruminate on them has wavered.

Sometimes…We'd be better served by being more reluctant with our mouths and more vigilant with our eyes!

Sometimes…When someone tells you they are thinking of quitting or breaking up with someone, in theory, they have already quit or broken up. Unfortunately, they continue to stay in that predicament out of fear of a lack of something better.

Sometimes…We need not be afraid of losing someone whose presence in our lives only leads us to losing more of ourselves with each passing moment.

Sometimes…The happiness we're searching for in our lives is in the hard work and the things we're avoiding.

Sometimes…We've wounded some close friends when we were younger, whether with our words or actions or our inactions. We never took responsibility and made amends for what we did. Most of these events can be chalked up to immaturity. However, just because we're not kids anymore, deep down we're still hurting and holding on to it. It's never too late to apologize. It took me thirty-five years to do so and now I'm free of it, and so are my 2 Mikes.

Sometimes…We make the mistake of playing a Russian roulette version of measuring our success and happiness in life to someone else's on social media, who's basing their success and happiness on someone else's, and so forth and so on. "Comparison Kills."

Sometimes…It's not how you sign your name as much as to whom, what, and where you sign it. When you choose to attach your name to someone or something, you're also signing EVERYTHING about you and your character to EVERYTHING about that someone or something as well. Choose wisely where you put your name.

Sometimes...You'll be faced with a difficult choice as a coach or an employer: character or talent? Choose character every time! You can coach/develop someone's talent, but there's no coaching up someone's character.

Sometimes...What we feed our bodies, in turn, feeds our minds. Processed foods are not only slowly killing us, but they're also slowly processing our thoughts, actions, and dangerous inactions.

Sometimes...When you think you are stuck, you're not. You either forgot how or chose not to move. Sidestep, front step, even a backstep—it doesn't really matter because any steps get you moving.

Sometimes...We encounter people who go above and beyond to drop hints of events, names, possessions, and places traveled in order to validate their wealth and status. If they were truly "wealthy" in their life, they wouldn't be trying so hard to disguise their insecurities. Plus, anyone who has achieved any greatness worth having also knows how difficult it was to achieve and how quickly it can be gone in an instant. Braggers brag because they didn't put in the work. They either deceived, cheated, or have someone to mooch off of, and if it all disappears tomorrow, they will find someone else to deceive, cheat, or mooch off of.

Sometimes...Anger only accelerates our lip movement beyond the speed of our minds and never builds or brings us anything. But anger can destroy and take away everything.

Sometimes...We all have had situations where people will just get up and quit on us. Be it a teammate, employee, friend, or even a spouse. The great lesson learned from all of these is to NEVER EVER take that easy road out and quit on yourself.

Sometimes...When we lose our temper and begin a verbal disagreement that escalates into an argument with a fool in the city streets, we risk that anyone who's watching might not be able to tell who's who.

Sometimes...Holding onto anger and our resentments of the past is like clutching a hot rock. In the end, we are the only ones getting burned. ...

Sometimes...We all know that someone who will tell us to "accept and be OK" with a particular situation when we know full well that if the script were flipped, they'd be raging holy hell!

Sometimes...Take a moment to appreciate the power of working with a purpose. It's always much more tranquil to strive for excellence when you are never bored.

Sometimes...The very last thing we just thought will be the very next thing we do. "Don't be nervous, don't miss, don't hit it in the water, etc."

Sometimes...No matter how justified a tardiness or a missed assignment, our circumstances do not change our responsibilities.

Sometimes...Our aura picks up on the negative and dangerous vibes of strangers before our mind catches up. Pay attention and listen.

Sometimes...It's ok to pray to God or meditate to a higher power as if what happens is up to them; regardless of that, ALWAYS work like it's up to just you.

Sometimes...We are so afraid of taking a few steps forward because all we see is a road ahead that's littered with all the hardships and negativity that consumes us.

Sometimes...Rather than being loved, seek to be valued, respected, and understood. It's possible to be loved and not experience the latter, but it's virtually impossible to experience the latter and not be loved as well.

Sometimes…You'll be criticized by people who are doing less than you, but rarely, if ever at all, will you be criticized by someone who is doing more.

Sometimes…The greatest feeling is to see someone push beyond their self-imposed limitations and smack that "f**k yeah" button, take a deep breath and a prideful look around, and then, on to the next climb.

Sometimes…You just got to get it wrong in order to learn and grow, and then…get it right!

Sometimes…Never let your mood dictate what you do. Take action and get moving. Movement changes mood.

Sometimes…Instead of caring about who's doing better than you, focus on making you better than you were yesterday. It's not you vs. them; it's about you vs. you!

Sometimes…When we avoid dealing with conflict in order to keep the peace, it just gets bigger and more difficult to deal with.

Sometimes…As we age, our ability to see people, places, and things becomes diminished, but our ability to see through other people's bullshit only intensifies.

Sometimes…It's not that I'm afraid of engaging with you chin to chin as much as I'm afraid of how much I might hurt you if we go chin to chin.

Sometimes…If respect for you or a loved one is not on the menu, it's healthier to push yourself away from a friendly or family table as opposed to being force-fed and ingesting more of what they're serving.

Sometimes…If some of the people you think are your friends don't miss you in your absence, chances are they don't appreciate you in your presence either.

Sometimes…Not everyone can deal with how hard it is to think, I mean, really think. That's why they just would rather pass mindless judgment instead.

Sometimes…You don't want to get up and walk out, not because you don't know the truth, you do, but because you want to see/hear just how good of a liar and manipulator they are.

Sometimes…The weak man always travels in a crowd while the strong man walks alone.

How Did We Get Here?

It's not mandatory to hit rock bottom in order to lose your ability to see; I was only halfway down when I realized I could no longer find me.

A beautiful family, accomplishments, and the accolades to match, but there was this lingering mental itch that I just couldn't scratch.

The tormented will always torment themselves in silence rather than speak their shame; we find plenty of other ways in which to hide and dull our pain.

My mind was clouded, cluttered and merely ornamental to the human eye, but my time out in the woods helped me face my demons and finally say goodbye.

Pen, paper, courage, and clarity are my new superpower, and the guilt and shame washed away like emerging fresh and clean from a shower.

The very last thing I thought I'd ever do is talk about the abuse that I hid; for now, these pages will only scrape the surface of all the evil that you did.

Sometimes…When you see someone by themselves, it doesn't always mean they are alone. It might just be they are strong enough to handle things by themselves.

Sometimes…It's possible to forgive someone without allowing them back into your life. Apology accepted. Future access denied!

Sometimes…People will be done with us because we survived the giant bus of lies and deceit they drove over us with.

Sometimes…You can become the absolute best version of yourself by putting in the work on the things no one can take away from you: being kind, being authentic, and being disciplined.

Sometimes…Just because someone appears to have many admirers and an abundance of friends doesn't mean that they are full of beauty, as much as they are proficient at costume changes.

Sometimes…Our words, our self-talk is our energy. Positive or negative, we absorb and harness that energy. Choose your self-talk wisely.

Sometimes…If an award were to be given to the greatest and most valuable player ever to play "hide and seek," it would be…The Truth!

Sometimes…We need to decide we are more than willing to adapt our lives to their absence as opposed to reconfiguring our boundaries to their contempt.

Sometimes…Don't be overly concerned with the folks who are always talking behind your back. They are behind you for a reason. Besides, what big dog turns around to acknowledge puppies yelping?

Sometimes…Look very closely at the friends and family around you and ask yourself one simple question: "Who in this room wants more for me, and who wants more from me?"

Sometimes…When all you do to build your brand is tell lies specifically to destroy someone else's, treat this process as a loan. Someday that bitch is coming due with interest!

Sometimes...When you cheated or intentionally hurt someone, and you think you got away with it, you didn't. True, maybe at the time, there were no repercussions, but karma has no statute of limitations.

Sometimes...If you are always giving and doing for others and not teaching them how to branch out on their own and create a name for themselves, they'll always be advancing on your name, riding your coattails, and possibly at your peril. If you're not careful, you'll be the one hauling that load for years to come. The eldest son has been dragging over four hundred pounds of ungrateful underachievers for almost forty years.

Sometimes...When people are always overly eager to help, remember that "help" is often disguised as the sunny side of control.

Sometimes...If you have reoccurring dreams about chasing a faceless person who occasionally turns their head to ensure you're keeping up, that faceless person is you. If they are running uphill, breathe deep and get to stepping. But if you find yourself seemingly always running downhill, dig in your heels and change the pace. Either way, our dreams can be the cheapest form of therapy.

Sometimes...The universe sends our exes (lovers or friends) back into our lives as a test to see if WE have really changed.

Sometimes...When you're watching a basketball game or soccer match (pro/college, men's/women's) and your child's favorite player just flopped or greatly exaggerated a foul or an injury in order to gain an advantage, that's a teaching moment! The fact is the player LIED. Yes, they lied, and not pointing that out to your child will open a vicious can of worms for them, not only on the playing field of their choice but in real life as well.

Sometimes...We all have two wolves running through our hearts and minds, each trying to conquer the other in hopes of controlling our attitudes and behaviors. One wolf is inequity and distress, and the other wolf is illumination and desire. The wolf that wins is the one we choose to feed every day.

Sometimes...Be humble enough to know that you can be replaced at any given moment, but also be confident enough to know that there is no one else like you.

Sometimes...Realize the person who just deceived or betrayed you did so on purpose (not a mistake), and in doing so just revealed how much of a cowardly person they really are.

Sometimes...You're either a wise man or a stupid man, NO exceptions! Wise men learn from their experiences. Stupid men habitually don't learn because they believe they already have all the answers.

Sometimes...Life's current issues, dramas, and obstacles are just like an erection. Sure, it seems pretty hard right now, but it won't last much longer.

Sometimes...The only thing a consistently negative mindset and outlook will give you is a life devoid of positivity.

Sometimes...If someone is always telling you they have a happy marriage, chances are you're not the only one they're trying to convince.

Sometimes...People who want to leave you first won't, so they will put you in a position where you will leave them. That way, they can spend the next few months portraying you as the villain and trashing your name and playing the poor innocent victim, garnishing all the attention.

Sometimes...No matter how hard and long we try, it's impossible to add more days to the quality of our lives, but we can add more quality of life to our days.

Sometimes...You just need to get to a point in your life where EVERYONE in your circle is wanted but not needed. This is nothing to do with love, devotion, or respect. But when we put ourselves in a position to need someone for our survival, we open ourselves to manipulation.

Sometimes...People who lack the ability to think with clarity and adequately communicate always see everything as an argument and not a discussion or a debate. They believe everything coming at them is an attack because they never take accountability.

Sometimes...Someone will tell you they find your personality and your presence intimidating. It's not your responsibility for how others react to your personality/presence.

Sometimes...A man who is a great fighter will win many battles, but a man who knows when to go to battle will not lose a single one.

Sometimes...If you consistently find yourself the smartest person in the room, find a new room because you're plateauing before you've had a legitimate chance to peak.

Sometimes...You've heard it said that when one door closes, another door opens, but not if you're repeatedly trying to use the same key.

Sometimes...It is perfectly acceptable to have so much more than you show and speak far less about all that you know.

Sometimes...If you start a business, one of the most disheartening things you'll experience is that, after everything you've empowered your people with, they still will not possess the same pride and effort as you do. You see them simply collecting a payday, and they still don't see your work ethic. That's because some folks are only capable of seeing others to the depths of how they see themselves.

Sometimes...That dream you've been dreaming alone may never manifest into anything more than a dream, but a dream we dream together can become so much more.

Sometimes...Be careful of the friends and family members who are always waiting in the wings to lend a hand because there always seem to be strings attached. EVERYTHING they do for others is weighted, calibrated, and documented for future returns on their investment.

Sometimes...The biggest cowards and creampuffs you will ever encounter will be those folks who pretend to be the innocent and harmless sheep in order to get into striking distance, only to reveal the true wolves they are.

Sometimes...Losing your temper as an adult is one of the most immature things you can do, and it's one of the ultimate public displays of weakness. If you are unable to control your emotions, you're showing EVERYONE in viewing and listening proximity that you are incapable of controlling yourself and maybe anything else that comes your way.

Sometimes...If someone is always telling you things they know about other people, chances are pretty damn good they are telling those same folks all the things they know about you too.

Sometimes...Despite what we may have been told, fear is not an action; it's a reaction, and courage is not a reaction but a choice!

Sometimes...If you're not quite sure about something you want to say or share out loud, say it to yourself first. If it sounds good and appropriate, open up and let it rip. If not, swallow it immediately!

Sometimes...It's ok if you're not initially the strongest, richest, best-looking, fastest, etc., because if you have the will to put in the work in order to become the very best you are capable of becoming, then you will be the strongest, richest, best-looking, fastest, etc. you were destined to be.

Sometimes...It really does just take only a few seconds of patience to avoid a lifetime of misery.

Sometimes...The absolute best way to gauge the quality of the person you just started dating is to look at the quality of the other people they have around them.

Sometimes...Friends will tell you they are "ALL IN" when it comes to a particular endeavor, event, or goal. Unfortunately, most of them have no idea what that means because there is a price to pay for admission into this club. Early mornings, late nights, skipping out on some fun things, being misunderstood and mislabeled, and accepting the fact you are both your own coach and cheerleader!

Sometimes...It's not always important to be the brightest candle in the room as much as the candle that stays lit the longest.

Sometimes...Some of the worst advice you will ever receive is "fake it until you make it" because some people will get to know, enjoy/love, and respect that version of you that's not really you. Eventually, perpetuating a version of you can lead to an inversion of you.

Sometimes...Mediocrity kills the human spirit. That's why mediocre people avoid high achievers and why high achievers loathe mediocrity.

Sometimes…We all enter and experience a comfort zone in our lives. But this is a zone only intended for temporary visitation, a place to refresh, refuel, and then move on to the next challenge. Far too many folks nestle in and never leave, and their comfort breeds complacency.

Sometimes…The majority of those who talk behind your back are doing so because you revoked their privilege of being able to talk to you face to face.

Sometimes…We just need to get to a point in our lives where we no longer have expectations because expectations are just disappointments under construction. Instead, institute requirements.

Sometimes…Telling a personal trainer or a coach of any type that you simply don't have the time is like lying in a court of law. WE ALL have the time; it's the priorities that we're lacking.

Sometimes…It's ok to walk through the wrong door as long as you turn around and leave, as opposed to getting comfortable and staying forever.

Sometimes…We just have to power through and figure it all out on our own. That's why some of the best advice ever given was NONE at all!

Sometimes...Take a moment and turn off the TV, put down your phone, and open a book. When you do, you'll turn off all the distractions, divisiveness, and anger, and open your mind up to some well-welcomed knowledge.

Sometimes...Folks never show their true colors until they're put into a situation and are forced to!

Shhh...

Can you remember the first time that you ever took a fall? Not a care in the world and no fears at all.

Deep down inside, we always knew that someone would be there, to catch or nurse us and render some care.

"You're ok" and "Go get 'em" were words and phrases we'd come to know, all designed to get us back up, dust off, and continue to grow.

Our falls became like a trail of dirty clothes left on the floor: bruises, losses, and heartaches always keeping the score.

But instead of a fall, have you ever been shoved? No one there to catch you now and to show you that you're loved.

This is not about playground bullies or high school theatrics; I'm talking about abuse: physical, emotional, sexual, whatever their evil tactics.

If you've been shoved, then you know exactly what I'm talking about; we didn't resist or fight back. We didn't even shout.

Broken bones, bruises, and cuts will eventually all heal, but we can never repair or replace the innocence that they steal.

It's rarely a stranger who inflicts all the pain but rather a "trust-worthy protector" who creates the stain.

It's a stain that never stops bleeding or makes any sense; it's a stain that we, the victims, pay all the expense.

All the promises they make are merely empty inside, a safe haven for all their true colors to hide.

We've all tried the same techniques to bury the trauma without a trace, but it's that fucking reel in our heads we just can't erase.

Sometimes...If we want to know if we're making a difference in our lives and in the lives of others, ask yourself this question: If I don't come home tonight or show up at work tomorrow, would anyone wonder where I am? Would anyone even report me missing?

Sometimes...You can lose a lot of money chasing women, but you'll never lose a woman chasing money.

Sometimes...A lot of folks seem to have issues with the whole "mindset" concept. They think that it's categorically impossible to change your situation by merely altering your mindset, and they are 1000 percent accurate. However, what they fail to grasp is by first creating a positive mindset, you ultimately change your attitude and outlook, which in turn immediately makes you better equipped to change your situation.

Sometimes...The people you know who seem to be constantly comparing themselves with others do so because they never take any time to realize, appreciate, and celebrate their own value.

Sometimes...Being on a winning streak is not necessarily the best thing, nor is being on a losing streak the worst. When we're on a winning streak, we have everyone else patting us on the back and telling us how great we are, which in turn can stunt our growth as an individual performer or a team. On a losing streak, you're isolated without fanfare and left to figure out and tinker with what's not currently working.

Sometimes...If you spend your days too fearful of stepping out and taking risks, don't fret because you'll end up spending the rest of your days working for and watching the ones who weren't too fearful to do so.

Sometimes...The most inspiring person you might ever meet is the one who is overcoming their fears in order to accomplish something and not the one who is already excelling at the same thing.

Sometimes...It's been said that those of us with too much free time and no purpose will always find and get into trouble. True, but a lot of those same folks also enjoy creating trouble and dismay for others even more.

Sometimes...When some of the people whom you used to know finally realize they no longer have any access to the person you've become, they'll just resort to trying to dig up the person you used to be.

Sometimes...Your character has but one language: "Protect me today, and I'll save you tomorrow."

Sometimes...When we want something that we've never had before in our lives, we must be willing to do all the things that we've never done before too.

Sometimes...We cannot save any relationship by giving them more of what they already have and don't appreciate.

Sometimes...Our enemies give and teach us some of the greatest lessons. They teach us who we never want to be like, all the things we don't want, and how, in the end, character reveals EVERYTHING about us for everyone else to see.

Sometimes...There are some simple truths and certainties in life: death, taxes, and the fact that if you don't make time for wellness, then illness will make time for you!

Sometimes...As parents, our shoulders are built to withstand the weight of our children's struggles, challenges, and hardships, as their shoulders will develop to do the same for the next generation. But at no time were children's shoulders ever intended to carry the burdens of the poor and selfish decisions of their parents.

Sometimes...When we take the time to sit alone and take an internal inventory of all the goodness and beauty we have in our lives, what follows is a genuine true love of self, and that results in no longer desiring to beat up and hurt ourselves, which leads us to no longer wishing to beat up or hurt anyone else anymore either.

Sometimes...We are faced with a path that appears we're about to walk through hell to cross over and get to the other side. If so, throw those shoulders back, head up high, and walk through like you own the place.

Sometimes...Some of the people who will travel in and out of our lives are like various parts of a rocket ship. There are a very select few who will have a seat with us in the command module and a host of others who are the rocket's boosters. As the rocket soars to new heights, some run out of fuel and detach. Not everyone was destined to soar to the same altitudes.

Sometimes...Anger is nothing more than sadness and trauma that's been locked deep inside without a way to get out...until it erupts.

Sometimes...An open window is what you make of it. Will you allow everything from the outside world to blow in, or will you toss out everything that's not working for you right now?

Sometimes...If you take any pleasure and satisfaction from watching someone else trying to weather their own personal storm, beware because your storm is just starting to brew!

Sometimes...We might get tired of the wrong person, but no matter what, we'll never get tired of the right one.

Sometimes...As a parent, we will eventually die someday. But we will live on in our children's lives forever. Will we be a cancer to them or a cure?

Sometimes...If we consistently expect more from someone than they are capable of giving and doing, then we will be the only ones who are ever left unfulfilled, hurt, and disappointed.

Sometimes...If you grew up in an abusive home, that's not your fault. But if you CHOOSE to raise your own family in that same abusive environment, then shame on you for wasting a painful but very valuable lesson and only passing on a curse!

Sometimes…When you're terrified about jumping, that's the absolute best time to take a deep breath and step off. When you no longer have a fear of jumping from that height, find a higher one.

Sometimes…The quicker you learn to respect yourself; the quicker others will follow suit and respect you as well.

Sometimes…Those who tell the truth will never be insulted by being questioned, but those who perpetually lie will always dislike being challenged.

Sometimes…ALL the choices worth choosing are hard. Choosing to be overweight is hard, choosing to get into shape is hard. Hard or not, the beauty is we have the power to choose.

Sometimes…It's been said that one day, our pain may become our greatest source of strength. But that also means that what we perceive our strength to be can one day become our greatest source of pain.

Sometimes…We MUST NOT allow the damaged families we came from damage the family that comes from us.

Sometimes…The strongest and toughest people we know are not those who fight right in front of us; it's the ones who wage wars every day in silence.

Sometimes...Some people will never realize what we bring to the table until they're seated elsewhere and get to watch us in action from afar.

Sometimes...We don't distance ourselves from friends and family to teach them any lessons; we do so because we finally learned ours.

Sometimes...Affection and admiration are beautiful things unless you have a relentless need to give and receive both.

Sometimes... "Men" excessively dispense a verbal vomit of things that don't match their actions. They are still little boys who like to babble.

Sometimes...Just because, for no apparent reason, a group of folks don't like you doesn't mean you should oblige and give them any.

Sometimes...Our pending success on the journey of achieving new aspirations is based on how we see and approach the day. Is it going to be starting someday, or is today going to be day one?

Sometimes...No matter how hard we try to keep something afloat or how badly we don't want something to end, we just need to pull the ripcord and land safely somewhere else. There's absolutely nothing wrong with starting over again because starting over again just means what you were doing before isn't working for you, and now you know better.

Sometimes...We need to painstakingly realize that just because we share DNA with someone doesn't always make us family; it only makes us related. Family is rooted in love, trust, admiration, respect, and the ability to disagree agreeably.

Sometimes...When we love someone else so much, we misguidedly put them at the top of the list of our everyday lives. Unfortunately, in doing so, we teach them we are only worthy as a runner-up. Regardless of where you are in life, you are NEVER anyone's runner-up!

Sometimes...We are going to be so excited to see some old friends and family from our younger years together, but soon realize a very hard truth: "Everyone grows, but begrudgingly, not everyone grows up."

Sometimes...There is nothing more rewarding than the ability to be free from some sort of affliction or injury, but for some, also nothing more terrifying than to relinquish a crutch.

Sometimes…You're going to find out that someone who you thought was a friend or even a family relative has been saying the worst things about you to other people. Don't be bothered with these people. Be more concerned with the folks they felt so comfortable enough with to say those awful things about you!

Sometimes…As much as we accept that we should turn toward our partners in times of struggle, that's not always pragmatic. However, the secret is not to turn away from them either. Our eyes were designed to see what's in front of us, and that's difficult to do if they are behind us.

Sometimes…We need to be aware that successful relationships have a five-to-one positive/negative ratio, meaning that for every negative thing that's done or said, research shows that we must do or say five positive things to counteract it. The power of negativity to cause pain and damage is stronger than the power of positivity to heal and bring us closer.

Sometimes…Every family is like its own band, and everyone is expected to pick up and play some form of instrument. Do we choose the instrument of an older sibling in hopes of shining brighter or a new instrument in hopes of shining differently?

Sometimes…We must understand the warning signals we receive must not be overlooked, because most warning signals lack the ability to tell us they can no longer warn us!

Sometimes...Just because someone is in uniform, teaching a class, or leading a retreat, doesn't always mean they are going to be honorable, trustworthy, and dependable. Kids wear costumes on Halloween, but some adults play dress-up all day, every day.

Sometimes...Some people we love and admire and who are supposed to protect and nurture us are the ones who end up hurting us the most. These animals of abuse have many faces (physical, emotional, and sexual), and they cut deep and leave permanent scars. They will ALWAYS warn us not to tell anyone and then make us feel like it's our fault or that we were asking for it! These transgressions are NEVER our fault, and we will never be whole again until we talk and tell someone about it. If we remain silent, we'll be swallowing the poison of their abuse all over again, day in and day out, all the while enabling them to continue with their depraved behavior.

Sometimes...No matter what has happened to us in the past, if we don't learn to love ourselves, we will NEVER be capable of truly loving someone else.

Sometimes...We might be sitting with an elderly parent, and they will ask us to grant them a wish while they're still living and breathing: a sibling truce! Unfortunately, there's just not enough glue and tape in the world to patch and repair the wounds to grant that wish.

Sometimes...If we don't take the time and necessary steps to heal from what or who has hurt us, then we will continue to bleed all over those who love us and have never harmed us. Others may do us harm, but it's OUR responsibility to heal ourselves.

Sometimes...Not all the psychopaths are in prison. Some are in our schools, our neighborhoods and workplaces, and yes, even in our own families!

Sometimes...There are the rare times when "the exceptions to the rules" happen. Broken crayons shouldn't be cast aside so easily because they can still color. I believe that with some assistance, support, and understanding, even pieces can become whole again. Conversely, some crayons, even the ones that are still intact, are just plain broken, and don't color anymore, and probably never did. Broken since birth, only knowing and doing colorless thinking and activity.

Sometimes...No matter how hard we try to forget or how hard we try to drink, inhale, or inject it away, trauma can keep us as a prisoner of the past and try to rob us and our families of the riches of today.

Sometimes...Men just need to let go and cry! Whoever coined the phrases "real men don't cry" or "crying is for sissies," I guarantee you died a very lonely and unrepentant man.

Sometimes...We're going to have to deal with bullies. They come in all shapes, sizes, and ages. The one who is consistently the loudest and most vocal is also the weakest and most scared. "As the wind howls, the mountain remains."

Sometimes...We just need to get off the "X" by whatever means necessary. In military terms, the "X" is the danger zone. This doesn't mean we're completely out of harm's way, but we're not sitting in it anymore either, and now we're taking the steps to find someplace safer.

Sometimes...We all need someone to vent to about our struggles and our issues. But quit sharing with anyone who's incapable of offering viable solutions.

Sometimes...It's damn near impossible to properly advise or understand someone without having walked a few steps in the same shoes.

Sometimes...The most beautiful gift you can give someone who is struggling is to just sit quietly and listen.

Sometimes...When we're doing our best to comfort or assist someone, it's important to know the difference between inspiring them to be better and enabling them to remain and continue the same behaviors.

Sometimes...It's never too late to have a happy childhood. You cannot fix or change your childhood to cleanse your mind, but therapy and exercise can help cleanse your mind in order to make peace with your childhood.

Sometimes...Although we have become comfortable with walking the path we're on, and it's hard to leave it behind, it's twice as reckless and dangerous to continue walking it too.

Sometimes...We need to resist the temptation to sit and break bread with those people who also choose to sit and break bread with other folks who intend to only do us harm.

Sometimes...We're going to be surprised how many people won't like the positive changes we've made with our lives. It's not that they're not happy for us, but they're now terrified because the spotlight of "accountability and change" is shining brightly toward them.

Sometimes...We need to do everything within our power to keep hatred from permeating our hearts. However, it is more than acceptable to see someone you used to know and care about and now feel ABSOLUTELY nothing for them.

Sometimes...People will do us harm time and time again. But we continuously make the ill-advised decision of giving them second chance after second chance when we really need to give them less means of entry into our lives.

Sometimes...We allow far too many people, places, and things to live rent-free in our heads. Regardless of the connection or relationship, for the sake of OUR own mental health, we need to start issuing some eviction notices.

Sometimes...It won't be until you're at your father's funeral that you'll realize you just lost the only man in your entire life that truly, without question, wanted you to be a better and more successful man than he was.

Sometimes...We all will have someone close to us leave this world. No matter the age, it always hurts. But one of the most painful experiences you will ever see is when you look into the eyes of someone who's licking their lips for the very last time and realize they have lived a life less fulfilled and littered with regrets.

Sometimes...We think our childhood heroes somehow mysteriously turned into villains overnight. But if we take a step back and closely examine their behaviors and body of work, we then see the signs of dishonesty, disrespect, and depravity were ALWAYS there in plain sight. We were just too close and blinded with childlike love and devotion to see it.

Sometimes...It doesn't matter if we scream because if we don't make a sound, no one can hear and help us. Screaming into our pillows offers only temporary relief. Stop hiding your wounds in the dark and concealing your fears in the light.

Sometimes...The only way to console or help someone heal who's struggling and is in pain is if at some point we have experienced similar struggles and pain is to share our experience. "Strength in numbers" is far more powerful than a lone wolf. When we help others heal, we are healing ourselves as well.

Sometimes...That guy at the bar or coffee shop with the big back, large biceps, and defined chest is not showing off as much as he's showing everyone he will NEVER be anyone's victim again.

Sometimes...You might be the one in your group that children gravitate toward, and restless babies easily fall asleep on your chest. Mesmerized, most other parents and onlookers will never know why that is. It's because these precious and innocent souls can sense in us our need to protect and comfort them and how, in turn, that eases the pain of not having had someone there who was supposed to protect and comfort us!

Sometimes...When we want to help others we care about, we tell them the truth. However, if we're only interested in helping ourselves, we just need to echo and repeat everything they're already saying.

Sometimes...It's not that we're not aware changes are in order or that we really don't want to make them. It comes down to the simple fact we really don't know if we have the discipline to execute the changes and our fear of the momentary suffering that's necessary to produce those changes.

Sometimes...The worst suffering we may ever experience is the things we create and manifest in our own imaginations.

Sometimes...It's not only easier but also much more amusing to identify and highlight the mistakes of others rather than concede to our own.

Sometimes...Some folks are flat out just not going to like us. That's on them more than it is us, and the only way for them to be "tolerant" of us is for us to be a little less like us, and that's a recipe for our own psychological disaster.

Sometimes...We will get attacked, not because we're weak, but because we pose some sort of threat to our attackers. We have something they want, but they are unable to achieve or earn it themselves. Burglars don't break into empty or abandoned homes.

Sometimes...We just need to get up and get to the gym and move some weight and replace our emotional pain with some physical pain. The physical pain of exercise not only makes us stronger, but a stronger body fosters a stronger mindset.

Sometimes...Certain people you encounter or even fraternize with are completely powerless without your reactions. Choose to preserve your energy and, quite possibly, your integrity as well.

Sometimes...When we come face to face with an old nemesis, it's not a battle between us and them as much as it is all about the "new" us vs. the "old" us and how we will choose to handle the situation.

Sometimes...The angst we felt as little kids on the playground, the terror of not being picked, and the horror of being left out only manifests as we get older.

Sometimes...It's not about who's always sitting with you under the umbrella on beautiful sunny days; it's about who's holding your hand as the rain pours down without the umbrella.

Sometimes...Only that one special person can hear what we're saying when we are silent.

Sometimes...When our employer demands we be at work by a designated time, we are. When that same employer gives us certain tasks to be completed by a specific deadline, we do them. But how is it that when we decide it's time to get into better physical shape and target the next morning to get started, we don't show up? Instead of a verbal or written warning, we allow this behavior to steamroll. This is precisely how and for whom the expression "being put out to pasture" was created.

Sometimes...Building the best body that you can is the ULTIMATE status symbol! No amount of money can buy it, and there's absolutely no way it can be borrowed or even stolen.

Sometimes...The people who have decided to leave our lives for what they envision as the "greener grass" will eventually one day return because they'll realize we are better for them than the ones they originally left us for.

Sometimes...If, like me, you have some fellow DNA shareholders who are habitually and painstakingly praying for your downfall, tell them exactly as I do: "Better pray a lot harder, motherfuckers!"

Sometimes…The people who are most broken and hurting are also the same ones that will drop everything to be there for someone who's in a crisis. They are willing to do whatever it takes to comfort and alleviate the pain because they know what that feels like. Unfortunately, these genuine and deeply soulful acts only leave them more broken because they know that no one is there and willing to do the same for them.

Sometimes…When we start to do new things in our lives, we may notice we no longer fit in with our old friends, and we haven't yet met our new friends. This space in time can be very lonely, but that's where our additional growth happens.

Sometimes…There comes a time in every boy's life when he acknowledges that he is all alone, and no one is rushing in to save the day. It is at this point the boy becomes a man. But not all boys will get here. Sure, they will still grow older, but their childlike behavior and tendencies will remain forever.

Sometimes…In many families there seems to be that one child with a different mindset, an agenda of sorts rooted in jealousy and envy and totally devoid of empathy. They were like this right straight from the womb. Over time, if allowed, they can tear a family apart at the seams. He did, he does, and will continue to do so. Toxicity behavior "from the cradle to the grave".

Sometimes...You're going to see the synergy between haters and cowards. The haters will always talk about you in a room until you walk in. Then they will morph into cowards and sprout a giant yellow line that runs up their back, from head to toe.

Sometimes...If you have ever had your love and loyalty taken advantage of and exploited, I'm sure you can destroy someone's world by telling the truth about the bottomless pit of deplorability they bask in. We don't because we also know the amount of pain and possible harm this may cause other family members as well. However, if, at any point, they begin to spin a different version of the events, I'm more than willing to open that book and reveal the villain's countless atrocities.

Sometimes...It's not the act of getting stabbed in the back that hurts the most. The real pain is when we spin around and see the actor in our life who's been wielding the blade.

Sometimes...Be the man who makes her smile and laugh out loud. If you can do this, you will beat out the man who promises to shower her with money and gifts. Unless she wanted money and gifts all along.

Sometimes…We need to get up and walk away from some people who are consistently disrespecting us, and they will respond by labeling us as difficult, a diva, or even a narcissist. They do this because manipulators despise losing access to the ability to play the role of Geppetto.

Sometimes…Take a colander and hold it under a running faucet until it is totally full to the brim. As soon as this happens, and not before, make the following pact: "I will now officially start investing my valuable time and energy into caring about what other people think and say about me."

Sometimes…No matter how much work we put into becoming the very best version of ourselves, we may still not be good enough for the wrong person. But no matter how far we fall into the worst version of ourselves, we're still good enough for the right person.

Sometimes…Too many people mistakenly believe that true love is all about grand gestures when it's actually the small ones that we don't even think about doing; we just want to do them and do them again and again and…

Sometimes…It's not the weight we lift that matters most; it's how we lift the weight that does.

Sometimes...The people in our lives might hold a board meeting in our absence to determine, without us, what's best for us. They may decide, without us, that the best thing to do is to throw away the worst of us in order for the best of us to come home again. In hindsight, if they took a little bit more time to think about what was best for us as opposed to what was easiest for them, maybe, just maybe, we wouldn't have gotten thrown away at all...

Sometimes...The places that were created to "help" us get better are merely circular conveyor belts in disguise. They are more concerned about making money and repeat business. Occasionally they get lucky and assist someone on the road to recovery, as long as your insurance says so and continues to pay. You can stay as long as you need to, or as long as your insurance says so and continues to pay. If you end up needing to come back, they'll be there with open arms, of course, as long as your insurance says so and continues to pay.

Sometimes...Just because we have friends, family, and well-wishers by our side doesn't mean we are still not alone. Too many of us take HOME for granted. Home represents joy, safety, and peace of mind. Whether by your own doing or at the hands of someone else, it can be a very frightening experience to be without your home for too long.

Sometimes...The conflict you're deferring is only multiplying in your absence.

Sometimes...We can become so fixated on looking at what we think is missing from our lives that we miss seeing all that there actually is. Where our attention goes, soon our intentions will follow.

Sometimes...The advice we are seeking and the advice we receive don't correspond with one another; that's because the advice they give leads us to where they are in life and not necessarily where we want to be or go in life.

Sometimes...We might find ourselves with someone who just doesn't understand what we are trying to say, but if we're lucky, we'll end up with someone who absolutely understands us without speaking a single word.

Sometimes...People who tend to drink too much on occasion are not doing so to get drunk as much as maybe just getting their inner gremlins a little inebriated enough in hopes they pass out so they can finally get some peace and quiet for a night.

Sometimes...We must acknowledge that unconditional love does not equate to unconditional tolerance of inappropriate behavior, disrespect, and abuse.

Sometimes...It's far too easy for too many people to become a "prisoner of the times" and join the "herd mentality" that, at the end of the day, accomplishes ABSOLUTELY nothing worth celebrating.

Hmmm...

I've often wondered why I always embrace the thunder and scorn the rain; the latter leaves rainbows, and the other only leaves me lonely and in pain.

I chose to chase bottles in search of peace and understanding, but I only found the liquid cure to be dangerous and far too demanding.

A lot of times, the glass was already empty before I ever took my first drink, and the only thing waiting for me at the bottom was more affliction and an impairment to think.

I walk around with an angel tattooed on my shoulder and vengeance embedded in my heart. My thoughts weren't always this disturbing; I was once a blank canvas ready for my work of art.

I was destined to be painted in vibrant colors, illuminating and ready to be seen. Instead, I was splattered and violated by a jersey of pale white and dark green.

The deviant, now decrepit, tipped things off as he was the center of attention. But it's the fatality of my adolescence that's feeding my distension.

I was victimized because I was smaller, gullible, and easy to manipulate and control. It's been decades, yet the mere sound of his voice sends me into a tailspin, and his septicemia still permeates my soul.

A perpetual rider of coattails with no kids of his own and all the traits of a little boy abuser. I'm a survivor, and he now shuffles with a stupor and will always be nothing more than a fucking loser.

Sometimes...Certain folks will tell you whatever happened in the past is just that: it's in the past and you need to stop holding a grudge. I tell them that it has nothing to do with a grudge, as much as I saw firsthand what type of person they really are, and I cannot unsee that!

Sometimes...We might find ourselves standing behind a steel prison door, hanging on with both hands while screaming to be let out. We're so busy screaming we don't realize it's not a prison cell at all, just a door we've imprisoned ourselves behind. We can leave at any time, but some folks are more comfortable with the prison they know than the feeling of freedom that they don't.

Sometimes...You know you're progressing on becoming the best version of yourself when you realize the one person with whom you have the least bit in common is the YOU from three years ago.

Sometimes...The absolute best self-care is choosing to be by yourself rather than wasting your valuable time, energy, and money on low-quality people who are simply not worthy of your presence.

Sometimes...If we continuously believe everything we think without question, we will be in a self-imposed prison. If we are always overly concerned with what other people think, we will be in their prison. At the end of the day, the sentence may not be the same, but prison of any kind is still prison, no matter where you spend it.

Sometimes...The absolute toughest part about feeling alone is not that we don't have anybody; it's that nobody has us.

Sometimes...All that emotional shit we throw up in the attic never goes away; it only disappears for a while. But like every other room in the house, eventually, we got to clear it out.

Sometimes...Creating a healthy body for longevity is like building your dream home. We start with a solid foundation, and then begin adding the walls, rooms, and roof. However, if we begin to add too many rooms or a second or third story, eventually the foundation will not be able to withstand the stress of the additional weight and begin to crumble and collapse.

Sometimes...Not everyone wants to hear about your current state of mental health until it manifests and erupts in anger. Then everyone is more than willing to label you as a problem, a bad person, or maybe even an addict.

Sometimes...We just need someone to validate our struggles and tell us how proud they are of how well we've managed to still hold on to all that is good about us.

Sometimes...A man's loudest cries for help is when he says nothing at all. We use silence not only to conceal our pain but to express it as well. In addition to his silence, listen to the music he plays, what he reads and watches, and how hard he tries to chase the pain away. People tend to say we are just overthinking things, when no matter how hard we try, we just can't turn off our minds.

Sometimes...Unlike the body, which immediately begins the healing and repair process when injured, the mind immediately begins the emergency response of protecting itself, by whatever means necessary.

Sometimes...You're going to entrust someone else with your heart in their hands, only to find out that when adversity hits, your blood slowly begins to sift through their fingers.

Sometimes...When you're told "it runs in the family," it's not always a good thing. Because if it's generational trauma, and you're not focused, it may just run you down and destroy all that you treasure.

Sometimes...In the deepest and darkest parts of the night, your eyes are going to beg and pray for some sleep. But your body will not oblige because it is knee-deep in a silent war between your head and your heart.

Sometimes...Become virtuous when choosing with whom you share your feelings, issues, and obstacles. The wolf will always come running when the sheep begin to cry, but they're not running to help.

Sometimes...We are all like books. Most will just glance at our covers, and some will only read our table of contents. But maybe, just maybe, you'll find someone who will turn each of your pages with breathless anticipation to see what the next chapter holds until you write your ending together.

Sometimes...We have all heard the old saying, "We're brothers from different mothers." But not everyone has heard the counterpoint to that saying, which is, "Although we share the same mother, you are no longer worthy of being called my brother!"

Sometimes...Teaching a child how to ride a bike is eerily similar to how we handle our own emotions and mental health. Do we run alongside, doing all we can to ensure a safe ride, or do we run behind, barely holding on till we give one final push off and hope for the best?

Sometimes...There is absolutely no difference between heaven and earth and the human mind and body. The storms and the fury from above can and will destroy anything that resides below.

Sometimes...Someone might ask us why we don't appreciate all the sunshine as much as we seemingly do the intermittent thunderstorms. Tell them it's because we love to sit and watch and listen, as nature also seems to have to scream and cry to calm its soul.

Sometimes...Passionate and soulful eyes can touch you so much more than any hands ever could.

Sometimes...Too many people only fall in love with the beautiful flower when it blooms but don't know what to do when the autumn of life rolls around.

Sometimes...They won't even think about crossing the street to watch you win, but they will not hesitate to travel across the state to watch you lose.

Sometimes...The most compelling move we can make with our lives is growing into someone who would have protected us as a child.

Sometimes...When some of the people we used to know realize they no longer have access to the person we've become, they will just resort to trying to dig up the person we used to be.

Sometimes...Some of the most beautiful flowers we have ever seen were grown with dirty water. Don't let the ugly people in your world and their dispensing of negativity derail your own growth.

Sometimes...It's truly sad to see someone choose the pain of holding onto something rather than the pain of letting the same thing go.

Sometimes...We watch/stream shows that some of our friends or family have recommended. But after the first few episodes, we're like, "I don't think so." They will tell us we need to stay the course because it only gets better, and it will be so worth it! Too bad we don't approach and handle building a healthy lifestyle the same way.

Sometimes...If we would simply invest a little bit more time in self-improvement, we'd have less time to critique or criticize anyone else.

Sometimes...Healing ourselves from trauma is not only the greatest gift we can receive, but to give ourselves as well. Because those of us who don't heal will approach each encounter and relationship and find some sort of offense. But a healed mind and soul understand that another's words and actions have ABSOLUTELY nothing to do with us.

Sometimes...A broken man will either face and conquer his demons or...he will become one.

Sometimes...The greatest generational curse is avoidance. It comes in many forms and only leads to a lumpy rug and a family of astute topographers.

Sometimes...Despite the depths of the things that have transpired in our lives, we know we're back on the right track when we refuse the urge to look behind us.

Sometimes...We all have bright times and our dark ones too. The bright times illuminate all we've accomplished, while the dark times teach us everything we needed to do first in order to see those bright times.

Sometimes…The healthier we are in mind and body, the easier it is to purge those from our lives who are not. It's like turning on the lights and watching the cockroaches scatter.

Sometimes…NEVER EVER let anyone who has never even taken a few laps in your shoes show or tell you how to lace them up.

Sometimes…If you don't eventually pick a day to get up and start moving, trust me, your body will eventually pick a day when you no longer can.

Sometimes…If we wait to do something until we're ready, we might never be ready to do that something.

Sometimes…Things are not nearly as personal as we make them feel.

Sometimes…The best things that have ever happened to us were at the hands of the worst things that have happened to us. But it's not always necessary to fall so low in order to reach so high. Friends and family are supposed to be that cushion in between. Unfortunately, those cushions mysteriously become deflated as we fall and miraculously inflate as we rise back up again.

Sometimes...We do have a tendency to overthink things. We do so because someone we loved and trusted in our lives hurt us, and I'm not talking about a little bit, but a lot! Some wounds are so deep they force us to be hypervigilant on protecting ourselves from ever being hurt like that again. This leads us to play out all scenarios in our heads about who, what, and where is bad and who, what, and where is good.

Sometimes...Even if both of our hands are filled with "glow sticks," everything will remain dark. Some things just need to be broken first before they can light up a room.

Sometimes...There will never be a shortage of them to stand and applaud our triumphs, but only that "ONE" will be there for EVERYTHING else that it took to receive those accolades.

Sometimes...It's ok to occasionally respond with a half-truthful "I'm ok, or I'm good." But NEVER EVER is it acceptable to respond with a disingenuous "I love you too."

Sometimes...We need to remind ourselves no matter how many times we fall or what mistakes or errors we commit, and even if our progression is slow, as long as we wake each morning and put our feet back in motion and keep trying, we'll always be ahead of everyone else who's not trying.

Sometimes…It will become painfully obvious we are excelling at the same thing an older sibling is doing when they become jealous and spiteful toward us.

Sometimes…Some people are only capable of finding you at peace and then leaving you in pieces. Thankfully, there are also those beautiful souls who can find us in pieces and help us again find peace.

Sometimes…It's not what you're capable of that matters most; it's what you're willing to do that does.

Sometimes…It's been said that the two most important days in your life are the day you were born and the day you find out why.

Sometimes…We must beware of the people who use the "hook of false praise" to manipulate their way into our circle because there is ALWAYS an agenda that has yet to reveal itself.

Sometimes…No one is more committed to trashing your name than the folks who are worried about you telling the truth.

Sometimes…We must choose not to sit and eat with people who we wouldn't choose to starve with.

Sometimes…The longer we neglect our issues, the more ferociously they dig and become embedded deep into our tissues.

Sometimes…Just because someone sends you mean-spirited, delusional, and dangerous thoughts doesn't mean you have to accept delivery.

Sometimes…There is no hierarchy to trauma. Pain is not worth ranking because trauma is not a contest.

Sometimes…Our partners become a direct reflection of how we treat them. So, if we don't like how they're acting, maybe we should look closer at how we behave toward them.

Sometimes…We need to apologize for the unhealed parts of ourselves that led to the hurting of others. It was never a lack of love for them, but a lack of love for us.

Sometimes…Anyone who tells you that we only live once is greatly mistaken. We only die once, but we get to live every single day.

Sometimes…If you and your partner enjoy going out to eat early and being back home by 7:00 p.m. and being in bed thirty minutes later streaming your favorite show, you're not old! You're happy, healthy, and forever in love.

Sometimes...The sad truth about relationships is that too many people are in love but no longer together, and too many people are together but no longer in love.

Sometimes...The best dream you will ever have is when you wake up, roll over, see his/her face, and know you are right where you are supposed to be.

Sometimes...The world is a place where monsters with pretty smiles are allowed to roam free, and angels riddled with scars pull themselves back up every day to make that same world a better and safer place to live.

Sometimes...The two safest and thus most vulnerable and honest positions a man will ever be in are either when he's in your arms or between your legs.

Sometimes...People will talk like they don't want to lose you, but their actions are telling you that they don't care about keeping you either.

Sometimes...You will never see a bee taking the time to explain to a fly why honey tastes better than shit. Remember that when someone pisses on your dreams.

Sometimes...at the end of the day, most of our children are going to start families of their own. It all begins with marriage. The question is: "Will they want a marriage just like yours or a marriage nothing like yours?"

Sometimes...The father we ultimately become is the one we really needed and wanted in our own youth.

Sometimes...Look them straight in the eyes and plead: "Please don't forget who I was and who I will be again and what we've had, have, and will have."

Sometimes...If early on you notice how he/she just can't seem to solve any problems, beware because they will become your biggest problem.

Sometimes...Little boys and girls are not traumatized by the act of being hurt; we're traumatized because we were left to sink or swim alone with our hurt.

Sometimes...If a woman truly wants you in her life, she will keep you focused and sharp as if you were her own, and she will debate, argue, and challenge you as a wife would/should, and then she will protect you as if you were her sister.

Sometimes...We won't initially appreciate it, but in the long run, we will realize those friends who allowed us to wallow in our bad habits didn't love us as much as those friends who called us out for it.

Sometimes...As much as we are the spark our friends and family rely on, we just need to get away from the people in our lives who never seem to have any, especially in the rarest of times when we need a jumpstart.

Sometimes...You cannot build a home with someone whos' not willing to carry a few of the bricks.

Sometimes...We are not the something that we did, but we will become the something that we repeatedly do.

Sometimes...We will be beyond grateful to see someone who we haven't seen in a very long time. We will tell them how much we've missed them, how proud we are of them, and how great they look. After a few minutes, we find ourselves simply staring at them and smiling as beads of respect start to spill from our eyes. Finally, we flash them the peace sign and slowly...step away from the mirror!

Sometimes...No matter what anyone else ever tells you, hope is a good thing. Hope is not the whitewashing of the things we've done or have had done to us. It's merely a lesson in curiosity and a realization that if we surrender now, we're forfeiting the opportunity to see what might be right around the next corner...

And lastly...

Sometimes...Flat-out refuse to hang your head because anything can happen. After all, anything happens all the time!

Zs of Serenity

I woke last night because I killed a man; I held his very last breath in the palm of my hand.

The fear and terror in his eyes only confirmed my truth; this grown man returned to defend his youth.

He's been on the lam since I was just eleven years old, euphoria in my heart as his body now grows cold.

I've wasted all this time chasing and paying the back rent, but my innocence was the only thing that ever got spent.

Divorced from his conscience and devoid of empathy, his nefariousness will no longer be mind-fucking me.

The road to perdition is over, and it is his to keep, so I peacefully roll over and drift off to sleep.

Matt McClure has been a certified personal trainer and performance nutritionist for over twenty-five years. He has amassed over 40,000 hours of training with a multitude of clients of all ages and walks of life. He has had the privilege to observe, listen, and learn from people with a wide variety of experiences, and combined with lessons learned from the obstacles he has surpassed, he's found considerable wisdom in his journey toward a happier and healthier tomorrow. Matt lives in Austin, Texas with his wife, and he is the proud father of two beautiful young men.